Being a Contented Christian

By Linda Singletary

Linda Singletary's books are available at special quantity discounts to use as premiums and sales promotions, or for use in training programs. To place a bulk order, please contact Linda Singletary at linda@lindasingletary.com.

ISBN-13: 978-1514386132

ISBN-10: 1514386135

Printed in the United States of America

Introduction

"But godliness with **contentment** is great gain."
I Timothy 6:6

It is the desire of my heart, and I hope of yours also, to be a godly woman. Not just a godly woman outwardly, but a godly woman inwardly. There is a difference. Many Christian women fit into a mold of doing what Christian women are expected to do, and they appear to be godly women. They don't participate in worldly affairs and they are faithful in the activities of their church. They are accepted as godly women, but in reality, they have only outwardly godliness. Their hearts may be cold, their attitudes may be wrong, and they are sometimes discontented and unhappy ladies.

There is danger in modeling our lives after other Christians. Christ is our perfect example, and we must keep our eyes upon Him and follow the directions given in His Word. It takes real commitment to the Lord to achieve inward godliness, but those who have inwardly godliness will have no problem with outward godliness.

I Timothy 6:6 says, godliness with contentment is **great gain!** When we can live a godly life, and be contented with our life, we will have accomplished much, and we will be pleasing to the Lord. These lessons will deal with the problem of discontentment and what we can do to become contented Christian ladies.

Linda
2002

All scriptures are taken from the King James Bible.

Other books by this author:

A Garden of Roses is Jesus

Being a Fruitful Christian

Being a Teachable Christian

How About Your Heart?

It's a Jungle Out There

The Beauty of Holiness

Walk in the Spirit

Wanted! Godly Women

Table of Contents

Lesson One

"The Demon of Discontent"

"The Demon of Discontent"

"...so the eyes of man are never satisfied." Proverbs 27:20b

We live in a day of discontentment. People are discontented with their jobs, their marriages, their financial situations, the way they look and just about everything in general. Discontentment is not a new problem. In the Garden of Eden Satan convinced Eve that if she ate of the forbidden fruit she would have a more fulfilled life. Her eyes would be opened and she would know good and evil. (Gen. 3:1-7) This looked and sounded good to Eve, but Satan failed to warn her of all the other problems this would create for her.

Even though discontentment has been around since the beginning of time, I believe it is much more prevalent today than ever before. Years ago people were limited to wanting what their neighbors had but now we are envious of what people on the other side of the world have. Transportation and communication have no doubt broadened our level of discontentment. Let's look at some attitudes that contribute to discontentment.

Unrealistic expectations:
In February 2000, my mother-in-law passed away at the age of 97. She was one of the most contented ladies I ever knew and I believe the reason for that was that she did not have unrealistic expectations. She enjoyed her simple life as a homemaker, cooking and caring for her husband and three children. She went to church, the grocery store and the beauty shop and spent time visiting with family and friends. She did not expect a lot of extras from life and she was contented with what the Lord sent her way.

Ps. 62:5 says, "My soul, wait thou only upon God; for my **expectation** is from him." If we follow this verse we will avoid a lot of trouble but many times our expectations don't come from the Lord. Hollywood has set the expectations for most Americans today – Christians included. We look through magazines or turn on the television and see things that we think we must have and we are disappointed and discontented when we don't get them.

Newlyweds often expect to start their marriage with a nice home furnished with as many things as their parents have while never considering that their parents worked thirty years to get those things. Couples spend every cent that they make on nice houses, expensive cars and all the latest gadgets, with the expectation that they will always have a good salary and that they will never get sick and have to pay doctor bills.

The problem is that salaries can change and sickness can come so unexpectedly leaving us in disastrous situations and very discontented. I once knew some people who were head over heels in debt. They received a large insurance settlement that enabled them to pay off their bills and they praised the Lord for providing their needs. Before long they were once again head over heels in debt. Instead of curbing their spending they continued to expect to own things and do things that they could not afford. This led to a lot of problems and discontentment for this family.

Wives often have unrealistic expectations about their husbands and their marriages. They expect their husbands to be perfect although they themselves are not perfect. They expect their marriages to be like a romance novel forgetting that novels are fiction.

A few years ago I met a fifty-year old widow with a small son. She lived on welfare in a low-income apartment complex and drove an old car. She was very unhappy and discontented with her life. She blamed her discontentment on problems caused by her second husband, but as I got to know her I knew that she was discontented long before he came along.

Her first husband had provided her with a lovely home and a new convertible car but he worked long hours and did not show her the affection she craved. Along came a man who showered her with attention and told her how beautiful she was. She divorced her husband to marry this man and then found out that he could not hold a job. They used up what money she had gotten from her divorce settlement then moved around the country going from job to job. They ended up in New Mexico where he soon died and left her with a small son that she was unable to control much less support. Her unrealistic expectations about marriage only led her into a worse situation and a more discontented marriage.

I recently read an article in the newspaper about the stress that today's children are under because parents expect them to be involved in so many extra-curricular activities. They are so busy competing in different sporting events that they have no free time to just be children. Many parents also have high expectations that their children achieve in these activities. This puts so much pressure on the children that they cannot enjoy the activities. Be careful not to over-extend your children or yourself.

I read a story about a thirty-year old retarded man who worked in a shop for the handicapped and on Saturday his dad took him to the airport where he got very excited watching the planes come and go. His brother, who had written the story, said that Kevin did not know that anything existed outside of his world of daily routines and weekend field trips. He did not know what it meant to be discontent. He lived a simple life without entanglements of wealth or power. He did not care what label was on his food or his clothes. He did not have unrealistic expectations. Could it be that we need to simplify our lives and change our expectations? Ps. 62:5, "My soul, wait thou only upon God; for my **expectation** is from him."

Unwise comparisons:
In II Cor.10:12, Paul warns the Corinthians about making unwise comparisons. "For we dare not make ourselves of the number, or compare ourselves with some that commend themselves; but they measuring themselves by themselves, and comparing themselves among themselves, are not wise." Paul's warning is about the danger of comparing ourselves to someone else in order to make ourselves look good.

We want people to know that we are not as bad as someone else, but someone else is not our yardstick. God's Word is our yardstick. There is also a danger in comparing what we have to what others have. This comparison can lead to jealousy and covetousness. God warns us about this in the Ten Commandments where He says in Exodus 20:17, we should not covet our neighbor's house, his wife, his servants or his possessions.

Heb. 13:5 says, "Let your conversation be without covetousness: be content with such things as ye have." Don't even think about comparing your husband to someone else's husband. Doing so can lead to more than covetousness – it can lead to adultery.

Don't compare your possessions to what others possess unless you are ready to take over their monthly payments. Trying to keep up with the Joneses can get you over your head in debt. If the grass looks greener on the other side of the fence, you can be sure the water bill is also higher. Be content with what you have. Don't compare your talents or abilities to that of someone else. Use what talents God has given you to the best of your ability and God will bless your efforts.

Another danger is comparing our blessings to the blessings of someone else and then feeling discontented, cheated or mistreated. Many times I have heard people complaining about how unfair God has been to them. The truth is that God has blessed all of us far more than we deserve.

Lam. 3:22-23, "It is of the Lord's mercies that we are not consumed, because his compassions fail not. They are new every morning: great is thy faithfulness." Peter became a little jealous of John, the disciple whom Jesus loved. In John 21:21, Peter questioned Jesus saying, "what shall this man do?" Jesus told Peter in verse 22, "What is that to thee? Follow thou me." He was telling Peter not worry about John but to be concerned about his own relationship with the Lord. Wasting time worrying about someone else's prosperity can cause us to have a bad attitude and miss out on our own blessings.

A danger for me as a pastor's wife for over forty years, was comparing our church to some big church and wondering why the Lord did not allow us to get bigger when I felt we were doing everything we could to make our church grow. I also sometimes wondered why another individual seemed to win more people to the Lord than I did when I thought I was being a faithful witness.

Many years ago the Lord showed me that I was responsible to work hard and to give out God's Word but He was responsible to give the results. The Lord wanted me to be faithful no matter what size of church we had and He wanted me to continue to witness no matter how many souls I won. Ps. 127:1, "Except the Lord build the house, they labour in vain that build it." In I Cor. 3:6 Paul says, "I planted, Apollos watered; but God gave the increase." Leaving this responsibility with the Lord freed me from a lot of discontentment.

We should never compare our prosperity to that of the unsaved. Ps. 37:7, "fret not thyself because of him who prospereth in his way, because of the man who bringeth wicked devices to pass." The unsaved will only enjoy life here on earth. We have all eternity to enjoy our rewards in heaven.

Unbiblical philosophies:

In Col. 2:8, Paul tells us, "Beware lest any man spoil you through **philosophy** and **vain deceit**, after the **tradition of men**, after the **rudiments of the world**, and not after Christ."

The world is being bombarded today with vain philosophies. They creep into our homes and into our minds through television and the teachings in the public schools until many times Christians are unaware that they believe something totally contrary to the Bible.

The teaching of the women's rights movement is a good example. Women are told that if they want to be happy they must first fulfill themselves. The Bible on the other hand teaches self-sacrifice and putting others first. Lev. 19:18 says, "thou shalt love thy neighbour as thyself." Rom. 12:3 says, "For I say, through the grace given unto me, to every man that is among you, not to think of himself more highly than he ought to think." Truly the way to spell **joy** is **Jesus, Others,** and **You**.

Another unbiblical philosophy that we see presented on so-called Christian television is the "Prosperity Myth." Many TV preachers teach that if you plant a seed by sending them some money then your money will be returned to you many times over. These preachers get rich while the person who sent the money becomes discontent waiting to receive something in return. The Bible does teach us to give and God does bless us for giving but we give because we love God and want to be obedient to Him, not because we hope to receive riches in return.

In Ps. 37:25 David says, "I have been young, and now am old; yet have I not seen the righteous forsaken, nor his seed begging bread." Phil. 4:19, "But my God shall supply all your need according to his riches in glory by Christ Jesus." God will provide our every need and give us many things above our needs but He does not promise to make us rich. I am amazed every day at how much God has blessed me both spiritually and materially, but I should give to Him because I love Him even if I never get anything in return.

In this lesson we have discussed three reasons for discontentment and some ways to resolve discontentment. There is no quick fix. God and His Word hold the solution and only as we spend time with Him in prayer and Bible study can we have victory over discontentment.

The Problem	The Solution
(1) Unrealistic expectations:	Look to God for your expectations
(2) Unwise comparisons:	Compare yourself only to God's standards
(3) Unbiblical philosophies:	Get your philosophies from God's Word

QUESTIONS

1. Three reasons for discontentment are: unrealistic _____,
    unwise _____ and unbiblical _____.

2. Ps. 62:5 says that our expectations should come from _____.

3. Heb. 13:5 tells us to be _____ with such things as we have.

4. I Cor. 3:6 says that God gives the _____.

5. Col. 2:8 says, "Beware lest any man spoil you through _____
    and _____ deceit, after the _____ of men, after the
    _____ of the world, and not after _____.

6. The best way to spell joy is J_____, O_____, Y_____.

7. David said in Ps. 37:25 that he had not seen the _____
    forsaken.

8. Prov. 27:20 says, "so the eyes of man are never _____."

Lesson Two

"Learning Contentment"

"Learning Contentment"

"Not that I speak in respect of want: for I have learned, in whatsoever state I am, therewith to be content." Phil. 4:11

When we speak of the demon of discontent do we mean that discontentment is a sin? I believe that discontentment is usually a sin, but not always. Discontentment is like a flag going up, indicating that there is a problem. On my mother-in-law's bedroom wall hung an embroidered work that she made years ago. It was called the Serenity Prayer and I have often wondered if these words contributed to her contentedness. "Lord, grant me the serenity to accept the things I cannot change, the courage to change the things I can and the wisdom to know the difference."

When we find ourselves discontented we need to first **identify** why we are discontented. After the problem has been identified we need to decide if we could **change** something that would help the situation. If we feel that changes are possible and profitable then we need to make them. Sometimes we cannot change the circumstances that have caused our discontentment. When that is the case we need to **accept** the way things are and make the best of them. We need to learn to be content. (Phil 4:11) We always need to pray for the wisdom to know the difference in these situations.

Discontentment left unchecked can lead to many sins. In our first lesson we mentioned the sins of jealously and covetousness, but there are other sins like depression, murmuring, bitterness and anger that can be triggered by discontentment. The list goes on and on. Sin is like a snowball. As it rolls along it gets bigger and bigger. One sin leads to another and many times we try to hide our sins and in the process only add to our sins.

In I Tim. 6:6 where Paul speaks about contentment as being great gain, he goes on to say that discontentment over worldly goods can lead to sin. Paul says in I Tim. 6:8, "And having food and raiment (clothing) let us be therewith content." In verse 10 he says, "For the love of money is the root of all evil, which while some coveted after, they have erred from the faith." Discontentment over money is a serious thing in the lives of many Christians.

If you have identified this as a source of discontentment in your life then consider why that might be and what you might do to correct it. The book of Proverbs mentions some reasons why people have money problems. Prov. 15:27 says, "He that is greedy of gain troubleth his own house." Some people are never satisfied. They always want more but getting more doesn't bring them satisfaction. I heard a man on TV, who the year before had won the lottery, say that he was no happier now that he had more money. In fact, he discovered that the more he had the more he wanted.

In Prov. 18:9, both wastefulness and slothfulness are mentioned as reasons why people have money problems and both of these are things that can be changed. "He also that is slothful in his work is brother to him that is a great waster." Prov. 24:30-34 goes on to say, "I went by the field of the slothful, and by the vineyard of the man void of understanding; and, lo, it was all grown over with thorns, and nettles had covered the face thereof, and the stone wall thereof was broken down. Then I saw, and considered it well: I looked upon it, and received instruction. Yet a little sleep, a little slumber, a little folding of the hands to sleep: so shall thy poverty come as one that travelleth; and thy want as an armed man."

A problem of discontent that young single woman often have is that of wanting to be married. Sometimes young ladies become impatient with God because He does not send them a husband and they marry someone who is not a Christian. This is never the solution to the problem. II Cor. 6:14 says, "Be ye not unequally yoked together with unbelievers: for what fellowship hath righteousness with unrighteousness? and what communion hath light with darkness?"

I know of two young women who have married an unsaved man and have regretted their decisions. Sometimes young women become bitter toward God because He has not sent them a husband. There are many things worse than not being married and one is to be married to the wrong man. Accepting your station in life will bring you contentment.

Have you allowed any of these things to cause you to be discontent? If you recognize one of these sins in your life, confess it today and ask the Lord to help you make a change. Even if you cannot increase your income you may be able to correct some problems that will help you to become contented with your income.

There is peace in knowing that I John 1:9 is still in the Book. "If we confess our sins, he is faithful and just to forgive us our sins, and to cleanse us from all unrighteousness."

Determine today that you will do something about the discontentment in your life. **Identify** the problem. **Change** and improve what you can. **Accept** what you cannot change.

I received an Email about accepting and enjoying life just as it is. I would like to share parts of it with you. Since I do not know who wrote it, I cannot give credit to anyone.

Happiness

We convince ourselves that life will be better after we get married, have a baby, then another. Then we are frustrated that the kids aren't old enough and we'll be more content when they are. After that we're frustrated that we have teenagers to deal with. We will certainly be happy when they are out of that stage. We tell ourselves that our life will be complete when our spouse gets his or her act together, when we get a nicer car, are able to go on a nice vacation, or when we retire.

The truth is there's no better time to be happy than right now. If not now, when? Your life will always be filled with challenges. It's best to admit this to yourself and decide to be happy anyway. One of my favorite quotes comes from Alfred D. Souza. He said, "For a long time it seemed to me that life was about to begin – real life. But there was always some obstacle in the way, something to be gotten through first, some unfinished business, time still to be served, some debt to be paid. Then life would begin. At last it dawned on me that these obstacles were my life." This perspective has helped me to see that there is no way to happiness. Happiness is the way.

So stop waiting until you finish school, until you go back to school, until you lose ten pounds, until you gain ten pounds, until you get married, until you have kids, until your kids leave the house, until you start work, until you retire, until Friday night, until Sunday morning, until you get a new car or home, until your car or home is paid off, until spring, until summer, until fall, until winter, until you are off welfare, until the first or fifteenth, until your song comes on or until whatever else. There is no better time than right now to be happy!

Happiness is a journey, not a destination.

At the beginning of this lesson we mentioned that discontentment was not always a sin. There are some things with which we should never be content.

- We should never be content to have sin in our lives.
- We should never be content with our lack of love for the Lord.
- We should never be content when we have friends and loved ones who are on their way to hell.
- We should never be content with this old world because it is not our final destination.

If we have received Christ as our Savior heaven awaits us. Jesus is coming again. What should we be doing as we wait for Him to come?

- Watch for His return. "Watch therefore: for ye know not what hour your Lord doth come." Matt. 24:42
- Stay busy until He returns. "Occupy till I come." Lk. 19:13
- Love His return. "Henceforth there is laid up for me a crown of righteousness, which the Lord, the righteous judge, shall give me at that day: and not to me only, but unto all them also that love his appearing." II Tim. 4:8
- Pray for His return. "Even so, come, Lord Jesus." Rev. 22:20

QUESTIONS

1. Phil. 4:11 tells us that we can _____ to be content.

2. Discontentment is a signal that we have a _____.

3. The three steps to learning contentment are _____,

    _____ and _____.

4. I Tim. 6:8 says that if we have food and clothing we should be

    _____.

5. I Tim 6:10 tells us that the love of _____ is the root of all

    _____.

6. Prov. 18:9 mentions two reasons why people have money problems.

    _____

7. List four things with which we should never be content:
    (a)_____
    (b)_____
    (c)_____
    (d)_____

8. List four things that we should be doing while we wait for Christ to return.
    (a)_____
    (b)_____
    (c)_____
    (d)_____

Lesson Three

"Our Father Knows Best"

"Our Father Knows Best"

"Thou wilt keep him in perfect peace, whose mind is stayed on thee: because he trusteth in Thee. Trust in the Lord for ever: for in the Lord Jehovah is everlasting strength." Isa. 26:3-4

Growing up in a small town in Ohio, I was eleven years old when I first saw television and I was disappointed in what I saw. It was very snowy with some figures vaguely moving around and I wondered what was so great about all of this. A few months later our family moved to the Cincinnati area where many people had TVs and I was very surprised to see there was actually a picture that you could watch. One of the early TV programs that I remember seeing was "Father Knows Best." It was a clean program about a doctor's family and of course, the father knew what was best for the family. How strange that concept is in many families today. It is also strange to many Christians that our Heavenly Father always knows what is best for us and that we should always accept His will.

Several years ago I started reading the book of Proverbs every day. There are thirty-one chapters in Proverbs and by reading one chapter each day (two chapters on the last day of the month when there are only 30 days) I can read it through each month. This has been a blessing to me and the Lord has used these proverbs to speak to me about many things.

One of the first things that the Lord dealt with me about as I read Proverbs was finding contentment by fearing the Lord. Prov. 19:23 says, "The **fear of the Lord** tendeth to life: and he that hath it shall **abide satisfied.**" To abide satisfied means to be content, but what does the phrase "fear of the Lord" mean? In the Scofield Bible the footnotes of Ps. 19:9 says it is "a reverential trust, with hatred of evil." A reverential trust is fear mingled with respect and affection. In other words, we respect God so much that we do not want to disappoint Him and therefore we will trust Him in every situation of life.

God is good and since evil is the exact opposite of God we should certainly hate evil. Hating evil helps us to love, reverence and trust God. To fear the Lord does not mean we serve the Lord just because we are afraid of Him or just because we respect Him, but because we love Him and believe He is **always good** and **always right.** One of the steps in the Serenity Prayer mentioned in our last lesson was that of accepting what we cannot change. In this lesson we want to take that point a step further by accepting that which is God's Will.

A few months ago a young woman came to talk with me about the problem of anger in her life. She knew that anger was a sin but she felt somewhat justified in her attitude. The reason for her anger was that she wanted to move out of their small apartment and buy a house and she wanted to have a baby. Her husband however, was in no hurry to buy a house and he was not ready to start a family. She was even beginning to wonder if he ever would be.

She loved her husband, was sure she was in God's will in marrying him and said she would quickly do it again. My advice to her was to accept God's will no matter what that might be. I felt that God would no doubt in His time give her both a house and a baby but I could not assure her of that fact. She needed to be able to accept and be content in God's will even if she had to live in an apartment the rest of her life and never had a child. She seemed willing to work on doing this, but I have seen many people to whom I have given advice agree with me and then walk away and forget all about it. I warned her of this danger.

The following week she returned to tell me that she was really working on accepting God's will and that her anger had greatly subsided. To make a long story short, the past three months have brought many changes in the lives of this young couple. They have moved into a lovely home and in a few months a new baby will join that home. It's amazing what God will do for us when we accept His way as being right, however we cannot accept His will just because we want Him to do things our way.

God's Way is always right:
Many years ago the Lord spoke to me because I was sometimes guilty of doing that. I always prayed for God's will but what I really wanted was for Him to make His will fit my plans. That is not the way it works. We must make our will fit His plans if we are to find contentment, because He is **always right** and He **always knows what is best** for us.

God's Way doesn't always make sense to us:

To fear the Lord means we will totally trust the Lord even when common sense points in the other direction. In Dan. 3, the three Hebrew young men trusted God even though they had been forced to leave their homes and had been taken as captives to a strange land. They continued to trust God and refused to worship the image even though they knew they would be thrown into the fiery furnace. They still continued to trust Him while they were actually being thrown into the furnace, not knowing that God would join them and deliver them from that furnace.

On over in Dan. 6, Daniel trusted God when he knew he would be cast into the den of lions. He did not know that God would spare him from those lions. In Gen. 6, Noah trusted God and built the ark when he had never even seen rain and even though he was mocked for believing that there could possibly be a flood. In Gen. 37-40 we have the story of Joseph, a man who endured many false accusations and yet continued to trust in God. Because he accepted these difficult circumstances he was able to do good work that rewarded him promotions and eventually led to his position next to Pharaoh in the land of Egypt.

We need this same kind of trust in God today even when we do not know what the future holds. We need to trust Him to supply our needs by giving our tithes and offerings and by paying our bills before buying things for ourselves. We need to trust Him by obeying His Word even when that is not the popular thing to do and we may be ridiculed for doing so. He will not fail to provide our every need if we totally trust in Him. When we accept that He is always right and His way is best for us we can find contentment in that knowledge.

God's Way leads to blessing:

When reading about the Israelites journey to the Promised Land in the book of Deuteronomy we see that they missed out on many of the blessings God had prepared for them because they failed to **believe** and **obey** God. In exchange for blessing they received a curse and a whole generation, except for Joshua and Caleb, were not even allowed to enter into the land.

The book of Proverbs is full of references about the fear of the Lord, but I believe Prov. 2:1-6 has the formula for how to fear the Lord. "My son, if thou wilt receive my words, and hide my commandments with thee; so that thou incline thine ear unto wisdom, and apply thine heart to understanding; yea, if thou criest after knowledge, and liftest up thy voice for understanding; if thou seekest her as silver, and searchest for her as for hid treasures; then shalt thou understand the **fear of the Lord**, and find the knowledge of God. For the Lord giveth wisdom: out of his mouth cometh knowledge and understanding."

If we will spend as much time searching God's Word each day as we would searching the world for hidden treasures then He will give us wisdom, knowledge and understanding which is what the fear of the Lord is all about. We sometimes have our priorities all mixed up. We think life is all about money and possessions, but Prov. 15:16 says, "Better is a little with the fear of the Lord, than great treasure and trouble therewith." Be more concerned about eternal treasures than earthly treasures.

For several years my mother has lived with me and gone to visit my brother for a few months each winter. Last summer she became ill and was not expected to live much longer. This made some big changes in my life style. I had been very active in our church and was always on the go. Now I was unable to leave my home unless someone was there with my mother.

During this time my husband resigned our church where he had pastored for nearly thirty-six years, and began to travel and preach in other churches. I wanted to go with him and wondered why God had allowed this to happen at this time. Not only was I unable to go with him, but much of the time I was not able to go to church at all. I sometimes felt as though I was being unfaithful to the Lord, but He showed me that this was His will for me at this time and that I was to trust Him and be content in the task that He had given me to do. I praise the Lord that my mother is better and I am now able to take her to church part of the time. I also praise Him for the lessons that He has taught me during this time of testing. The Lord has been teaching me contentment and preparing me for doing these lessons.

Many days my faith is small and I wonder what God is trying to do in my life. It is on those days that I pray this prayer. "Lord, I choose to believe that You are real. I choose to believe that Your Word is true. I choose to believe that **everything** that You do is right. I choose to believe that You have a plan for me and I choose to be content in whatever You have planned for me today." This prayer and this surrender of my will have certainly helped me to live a more contented life.

I suggest that you memorize Prov. 3:5-7, "Trust in the Lord with all thine heart; and lean not unto thine own understanding. In all thy ways acknowledge him, and he shall direct thy paths. Be not wise in thine own eyes: fear the Lord, and depart from evil." Many of you may already have memorized verses five and six, but don't neglect verse seven which is so important. Don't live in your wisdom. Trust His wisdom. Remember: **Our Father Knows Best!**

QUESTIONS

1. The Scofield Bible, in the footnotes of Ps. 19:9, gives a good definition for "fear of the Lord." It means _____ trust, with _____ of evil.

2. Prov. 19:23 says that if we fear the Lord we will abide _____.

3. The three Hebrew young men continued to _____ God even when they were being cast into the fiery furnace. Dan. 3

4. _____ trusted God even though he knew he would be thrown into the den of lions. Dan. 6

5. Noah trusted God and believed that there would be a _____ even though it had never before rained. Gen. 6

6. Even though he was falsely accused _____ trusted God and lived a fruitful and contented life.

7. Because the Israelites failed to _____ and _____ they missed out on the blessings God had prepared for them.

8. The formula for "fearing the Lord" is found in _____.

9. Prov. 15:16 says that the fear of the Lord is better than _____.

10. To truly fear the Lord is to believe that God is _____ good and _____ right.

Lesson Four

"It's Amazing What Praising Can Do"

"Amazing What Praising Can Do"

"Because thy loving kindness is better than life, my lips shall praise thee. Thus will I bless thee while I live: I will lift up my hands in thy name. My soul shall be satisfied as with marrow and fatness; and my mouth shall praise thee with joyful lips." Ps. 63:3-5

Several years ago a dear friend of mine went through a terrible experience. During this time we heard a chorus that had an impact on her life. It was entitled "It's Amazing What Praising Can Do" and as my friend began to try to praise the Lord she found that it renewed her faith and helped to heal her broken spirit. Over a period of time she was able to forgive those who had wronged her and has gone on to live a happy, contented life. She has developed into a stronger Christian and is a powerful witness for the Lord. Because of praise a life that could have been ruined turned into a life of victory. Though I no longer remember all of the words to that chorus, the title alone still helps me to hurdle many obstacles in my own life. Yes, it is amazing what praising can do!

In everything give thanks:

So many times when we as Christians go through a trial we murmur and complain about the terrible thing that has happened to us. When we react to the trial in this manner it only causes us to become more unhappy and discontented. I Thess. 5:18 says, **"In every thing give thanks**: for this is the will of God in Christ Jesus concerning you."** In our last lesson we talked about trusting God so much that we could accept His will in every aspect of our lives, but this verse goes on to say that we should also thank Him for every thing that comes our way. That means to thank Him for the bad things as well as the good things. This is not easy to do.

One day a lady questioned me about this verse. Her daughter was going through a divorce. She knew this verse stated, "In every thing give thanks" but she wondered how she could be thankful that her daughter was getting a divorce. Of course, she could not be thankful for the divorce but there were still many things that she could be thankful for even in the midst of this trial.

Her daughter was still alive and well. She had not suffered any abuse in this relationship and it had been a fairly peaceful breakup. There were no children involved. Her daughter had a good paying job and would be able to support herself. As she thought about it she knew that there were many reasons to praise the Lord. Her praise was a testimony which helped her daughter not to become bitter.

When I was a student at Tennessee Temple College in the late '50's, Dr. Charles Weigle, the writer of "No One Ever Cared For Me Like Jesus" made his home there. One day Dr. Weigle spoke in our chapel service about the subject of praise. He was an old man at this time and he had gone through many trials in his lifetime. In his message he kept using the phrase "praise the Lord anyhow." That night after the lights were out in our dorm a girl who was going through some trials of her own went out into the hall and yelled at the top of her lungs "praise the Lord anyhow." Of course, this startled everyone and she was reprimanded for her actions but that left an impression on me that I have never forgotten. No matter what the circumstances are we should trust the Lord so much that we can "praise the Lord anyhow."

Instead of worrying over things we should bring our problems to the Lord. When we come to Him with a thankful heart He will lift our burdens and give us peace. Phil. 4:6-7, "Be careful for nothing; but **in every thing** by prayer and supplication with **thanksgiving** let your requests be made known unto God. And the **peace** of God, which passeth all understanding, shall keep your hearts and minds through Christ Jesus."

Bless the Lord at all times:
Ps. 34:1 says, "I will bless the Lord at **all times**: his praise shall **continually** be in my mouth." Praise can have such a positive affect upon us and learning to praise the Lord continually can protect us from negative attitudes. Satan would like to take control of our minds but praise can keep that from happening. Satan would like for us to believe that God has forgotten us but praise can remind us that He loves us and that He is blessing us.

Praise can help us to see that the good in our life far outweighs the bad. In E.O. Excell's song, "Count Your Blessings," there is a phrase that says, "Count your many blessings, name them one by one, and it will surprise you what the Lord hath done." We take so many of our day-to-day blessings for granted and when we enumerate them we see just how many blessings we really do have. Each day as I have my devotions I try to write down five things that I am thankful for. This helps me to keep things in their right perspective and to appreciate what the Lord has done for me. My praises far out-number my problems and God is certainly bigger than my problems.

The joy of the Lord is your strength:

Last winter when my mother was very ill I was up and down with her many times during the night. Because I was not getting enough sleep I soon became very tired. One day as I was almost overcome with exhaustion I began feeling sorry for myself and wondered why God was allowing this to happen. The Lord spoke to me from Neh. 8:10, "The joy of the Lord is your strength." As I began to praise the Lord for His blessings to me – and I had many of them – I began to feel the exhaustion melt away. Not only did my praise bring contentment, it renewed my strength to go on.

Delight thyself also in the Lord:

Have you ever noticed how much easier it is to do something for someone who truly appreciates your efforts than to do something for someone who is never satisfied with the way you do things? This is also true of the Lord. He wants to bless us and the more we praise Him for His blessings the more He will bless us. Ps. 37:4, "Delight thyself also in the Lord; and he shall give thee the desires of thine heart." If you want the Lord to bless you then praise Him for the blessings He has already bestowed upon you. We are quick to call upon the Lord when we have a need but often slow to thank Him when He meets that need. Express your gratitude to Him everyday.

The book of Psalms places much emphasis on praise. It is good to read this book on a regular basis as a reminder to praise Him. In my Bible, I have marked all of the verses about praise, thanks, thanksgiving, joy, rejoicing, gladness, delighting, blessing, glorifying, singing and worshipping. In almost every chapter one of these words is used and as I read I am reminded to praise the Lord. By reading one Psalm each day the book can be read twice a year. By reading five chapters a day, it can be read once each month. You will be blessed by reading the Psalms.

Let's look at some of the things the Psalmist tells us to be thankful for:

1. His Word: 1:2; 56:4, 10; 112:1; 119:7, 14, 16, 62, 77, 92, 143, 174
2. His Works: 9:1, 11; 26:7; 98:1, 105:1-2; 107:8; 150:2
3. His Faithfulness: 92:1-2; 89:1
4. His Holiness: 30:4; 97:12; 99:3, 5, 9
5. His Name: 7:17; 9:2; 29:2; 34:3; 48:10; 54:6; 66:1-2; 115:1
6. His House: 42:4; 122:1
7. His Mercy: 31:7; 59:16; 89:1; 101:1; 136:1
8. His Benefits: 68:19; 103:2
9. His Salvation: 9:14; 13:5; 18:46; 20:5; 35:9
10. His Counsel: 16:7
11. His Provisions: 22:29; 63:5; 65:12-13
12. His Lovingkindness: 63:3; 92:1-2; 138:1-2
13. His Help: 63:7

These are just a few of the reasons we are to offer praise. As you read through the Psalms make your own list and determine to be more faithful in thanking the Lord for His blessings to you. We often limit our praises to those physical and material ways that God has blessed us, but we should also praise Him for who He is and what He does. When you feel low and discontented praise the Lord and He will lift your spirits. The time you least feel like praising the Lord is the time you need to praise Him the most. **It is amazing what praising can do!**

The following is a short poem of praise I wrote back in 1984, while traveling through the beautiful state of Tennessee.

Thank You

Lord, thank you for the wonders that I saw today.
The sun that shone so bright above the earth;
The blue sky filled with fluffy, floating clouds;
The rolling hills with lush green grass and trees;
The winding stream and sparkling waterfall;
The deer that ran across the road;
I thank you, Lord, for all of these and more.

QUESTIONS

1. I Thess. 5:18 says that we are to give thanks for _____.

2. Does this mean to give thanks for the bad things as well as the good? _____

3. What added blessing does God promise us in Phil 4:6 if our requests are made with a thankful heart? _____

4. How often should we offer praise? _____ Ps. 34:1

5. Neh. 8:10 tells us that the joy of the Lord is our _____.

6. Ps. 37:4 says that if we delight ourselves in the Lord, He will give us the

   _____

7. List six things that the Psalmist tell us to be thankful for.

   _____

   _____

   _____

   _____

   _____

   _____

Lesson Five

"Love is a Choice"

"Love is a Choice"

"What doth the Lord thy God require of thee, but to fear the Lord thy God, to walk in all his ways, and to love him, and to serve the Lord thy God with all thy heart and with all thy soul." Deut. 10:12

As a young bride with stars in my eyes I believed that a person fell in love and was hopelessly unable to do anything about it. I disagreed with my husband who said that love is a choice, but as I matured and learned God's Word I realized that he was right. God requires us to make a choice as to whether or not we will love Him. (Deut. 10:12) In order to be saved we must love Him and in order to be obedient to Him we must love others. Matt. 22:37-39, "Jesus said unto him, Thou shalt **love** the Lord thy God with all thy heart, and with all thy soul, and with all thy mind." This is the first and great commandment. And the second is like unto it, Thou shalt **love** thy neighbour as thyself."

A young wife with four children once came to me for counsel. She was discontented in her marriage, no longer loved her husband and was ready to get a divorce. Her husband had not mistreated her or been unfaithful to her, but he did not show her the attention and affection that she desired. I talked to her about love being a choice and that if she had once loved her husband enough to marry him then she could choose to love him again and stay married to him. By her doing her part I felt that she could rekindle the love in her husband and save her marriage. Even though she agreed with me at the time she did not choose to take my advice. The marriage ended in a divorce and those precious children were badly hurt by her choice.

In John 21 we read the story of how after Jesus had risen from the dead he was not always with the disciples. He did appear to them on occasions, one of which was at the sea of Tiberias. Peter may have been somewhat discontent with this new way of life. He had been used to being with Jesus, hearing Him preach, and seeing Him perform miracles every day. He decided to go back to his fishing and some of the other disciples went along, but after fishing all night they had caught nothing. It was then that Jesus appeared on the shore and told them to cast their nets on the other side of the ship.

When they obeyed their nets became full of fish. Jesus invited them to dine on the fish he had already prepared for them. After they had dined Jesus asked Peter if he loved Him. Peter replied that he did, but Jesus evidently was not satisfied with his answer and asked him two more times. Each time when Peter said that he did, Jesus told him to feed His lambs or His sheep. If Peter could love the Lord more than anything else then he would be able to be content in the job that God had called him to do.

As Christians, God has given us all jobs to do and we need to be content in whatever our job is. If you are a wife and a mother you have an obligation to love your family. If you are a Sunday School teacher you have an obligation to love your class. Whatever God has called you to do He can enable you to do it with contentment in your heart. Love is a vital part of contentment and we see a lack of both love and contentment today.

The Bible warns us that in the last days that would happen. Matt. 24:12, "And because iniquity shall abound, the love of many shall wax cold." In this verse Christ was speaking to believers. We are not exempt from this problem. In speaking to the church at Ephesus John praises them for their good works but says, "Nevertheless I have somewhat against thee, because thou hast left thy first love." (Rev. 2:4) Think back to those days when you first fell in love with your husband. Think back to the days when you first got saved. How is your love life today? If your love has waxed cold you are no doubt also having a problem with contentment.

Self Love:
Earlier we mentioned the unbiblical philosophy of loving ourselves and putting ourselves above others. We are being taught today that we must first love ourselves in order to love others, but the Bible teaches us to love God first and to love others second. (Mark 12:28-31) I Cor. 13:4-5 says "**charity** (another word for love) **vaunteth not itself, is not puffed up. Doth not behave itself unseemly, seeketh not her own**." It is true that we need to accept ourselves as God made us, but to love ourselves above others can be very dangerous.

Pride is a result of self-love and Proverbs has much to say about the dangers of pride. Prov. 6:16-17 lists pride as one of the things that God hates. Prov. 11:2 says, "When pride cometh, then cometh shame;" Prov. 15:25, "The Lord will destroy the house of the proud:" Prov. 16:5, "Every one that is proud in heart is an abomination to the Lord:" Prov. 16:18, "Pride goeth before destruction," Prov. 21:4, "a proud heart.....is sin." Prov. 29:23, "A man's pride shall bring him low:" God is not happy with pride and if we live a life of self-love and pride we will definitely not be happy and contented with ourselves.

Worldly Love:

I John 2:15-16, "Love not the world, neither the things that are in the world, If any man love the world, the love of the Father is not in him. For all that is in the world, the **lust of the flesh**, and the **lust of the eyes**, and the **pride of life**, is not of the Father, but is of the world." When God tells us not to love the world He is not speaking of the people in the world but rather of the world system and its philosophies. The world's concept of love is lust. Lust is satisfying self while love is seeking to satisfy someone else. How ironical it is that to satisfy or fulfill someone else can also be very fulfilling and satisfying to us.

God's Love:

Not only is God a perfect example of what love is and of how to love, but I John 4:8 tells us "God is love." How did God reveal His love to us? I John 4:9-10, "In this was manifested the love of God toward us, because that God sent his only begotten Son into the world, that we might live through him. Herein is love, not that we loved God, but that he loved us, and sent his Son to be the propitiation for our sins."

Loving God:

We should be so grateful to Him for providing a way of salvation and deliverance from hell that we would receive Him as our Saviour and make Him the Lord of our life. I John 4:19, "We love him, because he first loved us." We did nothing to deserve His love but He loved us just the same. Accepting His love places His love in us and causes us to love Him in return.

To love God is to love His Word: Ps. 119:97, "O how love I thy law! it is my meditation all the day." Ps. 119:127, "I love thy commandments above gold; yea, above fine gold." Ps. 119:165, "Great peace have they that love thy law." To love His Word is to obey His Word. Isa.48:18, "O that thou hadst hearkened to my commandments! then had thy peace been as a river, and thy righteousness as the waves of the sea:" Loving and obeying God's Word brings peace which goes hand in hand with contentment.

To love God is to love His House: Ps. 26:8, "Lord, I have loved the habitation of thy house, and the place where thine honor dwelleth." Ps. 122:1 "I was glad when they said unto me, Let us go into the house of the Lord." We show our love for the Lord by wanting to spend time fellowshipping with Him in His Word and in His House.

Loving others:

To love God is to love others. I John 4:7-8, "Beloved, let us love one another: for love is of God; and every one that loveth is born of God, and knoweth God. He that loveth not knoweth not God." Verse 11, "Beloved, if God so loved us, we ought also to love one another." Just as we are often not deserving of God's love our friends may not be deserving of our love, but we are to love them just the same. Prov. 17:17 says, "A friend loveth at all times."

The old saying, "love is blind" is very true. When couples are first in love they often fail to see the faults the other one possesses. Having God's love can blind us to the faults of others. Prov. 10:12, "...love covereth all sins." I Pet. 4:8, "And above all things have fervent charity among yourselves: for charity shall cover the multitude of sins." The greatest joy comes from giving to others and the most satisfying work is that of helping others. The powerful force that makes these two things possible is love.

I Cor. 13:7 says that love "endureth all things." Shortly after moving to Albuquerque in 1967, my husband became very ill. We were expecting our third child and when our new baby girl was only three weeks old the doctor did exploratory surgery and found that my husband had pancreatic cancer.

We were given little hope that he would survive the surgery much less live for any period of time. But God had other plans and now thirty-five years later my husband is still going strong. Praise God our love endured the test of illness and some financial tests that accompanied that illness. In fact, these trials helped to strengthen our love for each other and for the Lord.

I Cor. 13 is known as the great Love chapter. It tells us that without love we are nothing. I Cor. 13:4-8, tells us how to identify real love. "Charity suffereth long, and is kind; charity envieth not; charity vaunteth not itself, is not puffed up. Doth not behave itself unseemly, seeketh not her own, is not easily provoked, thinketh no evil; Rejoiceth not in iniquity, but rejoiceth in the truth; Beareth all things, believeth all things, hopeth all things, endureth all things. Charity never faileth." This is the kind of love that God has and that He wants us as Christians to have.

How is it possible to have this kind of love?

- Accept God's love. John 3:16, "For God so loved the world, that he gave his only begotten Son, that whosoever believeth in him should not perish, but have everlasting life.
- Allow Him to perfect His love in you. I John 4:12b, "If we love one another, God dwelleth in us, and his love is perfected in us."
- Appropriate the help of the Holy Spirit. I John 4:13, "Hereby know we that we dwell in him, and he in us, because he hath given us of his Spirit."
- Act in obedience to His Word. I John 2:5, "But whoso keepeth his word, in him verily is the love of God perfected: hereby know we that we are in him." John 15:10, "If ye keep my commandments, ye shall abide in my love."

In the Sermon on the Mount Christ goes a step further and says, "Ye have heard that it hath been said, Thou shalt love thy neighbour, and hate thine enemy. But I say unto you, Love your enemies, bless them that curse you, do good to them that hate you, and pray for them which despitefully use you, and persecute you:" With the help of the Holy Spirit even this is possible.

Love is necessary for living a contented life. To be content in our service for the Lord we must love God above everything else. To be content in our marriage we must love our husband unreservedly. To be content in our home we must love our children unconditionally. To be content in our church we must love our fellow church members. To be content on our job we must love our co-workers as well as our boss.

Not only is love a choice but to choose to love is the greatest choice that we can make. **I Cor. 13:13, "And now abideth faith, hope, charity, these three; but the greatest of these is charity."**

QUESTIONS

1. What is the first and great commandment given in Matt. 22:37?

    _____

2. What is the second commandment like unto the first?

    _____

3. In John 21, how many times did Jesus ask Peter if he loved him? _____

4. I Cor. 13:4-5 tells us that love is not _____ and seeketh not her _____.

5. The world's idea of love is _____.

6. How did God manifest His love to us? _____

    I John 4:9

7. I John 4:8 says "He that loveth not _____ God."

8. Prov. 17:17 says "A friend loveth at _____."

9. List four things that can help us to love as God loves.

    _____

    _____

    _____

    _____

The Wondrous Love of Jesus

O, the wondrous love of Jesus,
It is far beyond compare,
And the thing that's so amazing is
His love is everywhere.
It reaches from the highest mountain,
To the islands of the sea;
To the deepest, darkest valley;
And, praise God, His love is free.

Love beyond all comprehension,
It can cover any sin,
It can change the vilest sinner,
Make him pure without, within.
And this love has yet no limits,
It can set the captive free,
It can mend the broken-hearted,
Still there's love enough for me.

Coda:
O, I'm on my way to heaven,
I've been redeemed by Jesus' blood.
All my sins have been forgiven,
Just because of His great love.

Linda Singletary

Lesson Six

"Abiding in Him"

"Abiding in Him"

"These things have I spoken unto you, that my joy might remain in you, and that your joy might be full." John 15:11

Do you remember the early days of being in love and how you wanted to spend every available minute with the one you loved? When my husband and I started dating I was teaching school in Florida. I couldn't wait to get home from school each afternoon because I knew that soon after I arrived home he would call. Most evenings he also came to see me. We did not have money to go many places but we enjoyed just being together and talking.

After over forty years of marriage I still enjoy spending time with my husband. In recent months he has been away preaching quite a lot. Because I care for my aging mother I am usually unable to accompany him. When he is gone I look forward to his daily calls and I am excited when he comes home. I want to spend time with him. Today I know my husband far better than I did the day I married him back in 1960. Spending time with him has helped me to get to know him. The same is true with the Lord, the more time I spend with Him the better I get to know Him, and the better I know Him the easier it is to love Him, trust Him and obey Him.

Abiding in the Vine:

John 15 is a great chapter about the necessity of abiding in Christ. Just as the branches must stay connected to the vine in order to bear fruit, we must stay connected to the Lord if we are to be fruitful Christians. John 15:5, "I am the vine, ye are the branches: He that **abideth** in me, and I in him, the same bringeth forth much fruit: for without me ye can do nothing." To abide in the Lord is not just reading a chapter from the Bible each day, it is more than praying before you eat a meal and it is more than attending church every Sunday. To abide means to continue with the Lord all day and every day. We should read God's Word every day, and throughout the day we should meditate on what we have read. Ps. 1:2, "But his **delight** (another form of contentment) is in the law of the Lord; and in his law doth he **meditate** day and night."

One of the conditions for answered prayer is to abide in Christ. John 15:7, "If ye **abide** in me, and my words **abide** in you, ye shall ask what ye will, and it shall be done unto you." To abide in the Lord is not to pray just when we have a need, but to continue in an attitude of prayer throughout the day. I Thess. 5:17 tells us to,

"Pray without ceasing." We do not have to be on our knees to pray. Abiding Christians talk to the Lord just as they would to a friend – at any time, at any place and about anything.

Abiding by the Waters:

Ps. 1:3 goes on to say, "And he shall be like a tree **planted** by the rivers of water, that bringeth forth his fruit in his season; his leaf also shall not wither; and whatsoever he doeth shall prosper." Jer. 17:7-8 says, "Blessed is the man that trusteth in the Lord, and whose hope the Lord is. For he shall be as a tree planted by the waters, and that spreadeth out her roots by the river, and shall not see when heat cometh, but her leaf shall be green; and shall not be careful in the year of drought, neither shall cease from yielding fruit."

Driving through New Mexico on interstate 25 you see a perfect example of being planted by the waters. The interstate is not far from the Rio Grande and even though that is a very small river you can see a strip of green along the river that is such a contrast to the land on the other side of the road. Being planted by the waters does make a difference in the vegetation. When we are thirsty for God and stay planted in His Word, it will make a difference in our lives. We will become fruitful, contented Christians. Ps. 107:9, "For he satisfieth the longing soul, and filleth the hungry soul with goodness."

Abiding under His Wings:

Ps. 91:1-4, "He that dwelleth in the secret place of the most High shall **abide** under the shadow of the Almighty. I will say of the Lord, He is my refuge and my fortress: my God; in him will I trust. Surely he shall deliver thee from the snare of the fowler, and from the noisome pestilence. He shall cover thee with his feathers, and under his wings shalt thou trust: his truth shall be thy shield and buckler." The closer we stay to the Lord and the more we abide in the Lord the more protected we will be from the traps of sin that surround us every day.

In Matt. 23:37 Jesus laments over Jerusalem, "O Jerusalem, Jerusalem, thou that killest the prophets, and stonest them which are sent unto thee, how often would I have gathered thy children together, even as a hen gathereth her chickens under her wings, and ye would not!"

He must also lament over Christians who will not spend time with Him. His arms of protection are open to us, but we must enter into them to receive that protection and the satisfaction that protection brings.

Abiding for Joy:
The Bible gives us instructions about abiding so that we might become joyful and contented Christians. John 15:11, "These things have I spoken unto you, that **my joy** might remain in you, and that **your joy** might be full." Some of my most contented moments are when I am spending time in God's Word and fellowshipping with Him. It is sad to say, but not every time that I read my Bible do I have this contentment and joy. That is not God's fault – it is mine. Many days I hurriedly read His Word and my mind is somewhere else. This is not abiding in Him. It is important that I clear my mind and give God my undivided attention if I am to abide in Him.

We all dream of how satisfying it would be to go on a vacation to some exotic resort. The Bible tells us that we can enjoy this satisfaction everyday by simply getting alone with the Lord. Ps. 71:3, "Be thou my strong habitation, whereunto I may continually resort:" During the summer months my backyard is the place where I resort. I call it my sanctuary, because even though I live in the city, it is a quiet place where I spend time with the Lord. We need a quiet place free from distractions where we can meditate on His Word and abide in Him. Ps. 46:10, "Be still and know that I am God." Isa. 30:15b, "...in quietness and in confidence shall be your strength:"

Mary, the sister of Martha and Lazarus, was a good example of someone who was constantly abiding with the Lord. Every time she is mentioned in the Bible she is at the feet of Jesus. In Lk. 10:39 she "...**sat at Jesus' feet, and heard his word**." While Martha served Mary sat and listened. Service is certainly an important part of the Christian life but it should always follow sitting at Jesus' feet.

In John 11:32 "**she fell down at his feet**, saying unto him, Lord, if thou hadst been here, my brother had not died." Falling at Jesus' feet was an act of humility and of worship. Mary wept as she knelt at His feet and Jesus responded by weeping with her.

Again in John 12:3, Mary displayed humility and worship. "Then took Mary a pound of ointment of spikenard, very costly, and **anointed the feet of Jesus,** and wiped his feet with her hair:" This act also revealed sacrifice. Mary must have saved for a long time to buy this ointment. Judas was upset by her extravagance and said this ointment could have been sold and the money given to the poor. Of course, he intended to put it into his own pocket. But Jesus was not upset at Mary's deed and said that she had helped to prepare Him for his burying. Jesus commended Mary for her devotion and sacrifice by saying in John 12:8, "For the poor always ye have with you; but me ye have not always."

We live such busy lives today. It is so difficult to find time to spend with the Lord, but if we don't take time to abide with Him today, when will we ever do it? Just as Mary sacrificed to buy the ointment that she poured on Jesus' feet so we must sacrifice our time if we are to abide in Him. If we are ever to do anything of value for the Lord we must spend time at Jesus' feet just as Mary did. When we abide in the Lord we will have no trouble trusting the Lord, obeying the Lord, praising the Lord or loving the Lord. Have you been abiding in the Lord? If we are to be godly contented women we must abide in the Lord.

"But godliness with contentment is great gain."
I Timothy 6:6

QUESTIONS

1. John 15:5 tells us if we want to be fruitful contented Christians we must

   _____.

2. Ps. 1:2 tells us to _____ in God's law day and night.

3. According to John 15:7, one of the conditions for answered prayer is to

   _____.

4. One of the benefits of abiding in the Lord is _____.

   Ps. 91:1-4

5. Jesus tells us in John 15:11 that He wants our joy to be _____.

6. Give an example of someone who was constantly abiding with the Lord

   _____

7. Mary at Jesus' feet showed three things, _____,

   _____ and _____.

8. Godliness with contentment is great _____.

Made in the USA
San Bernardino, CA
16 April 2016